Confident Reader titles are ideal for children who are developing greater reading confidence and stamina, and can independently read simple stories with a wider vocabulary.

Special features:

Wider vocabulary, reinforced through repetition

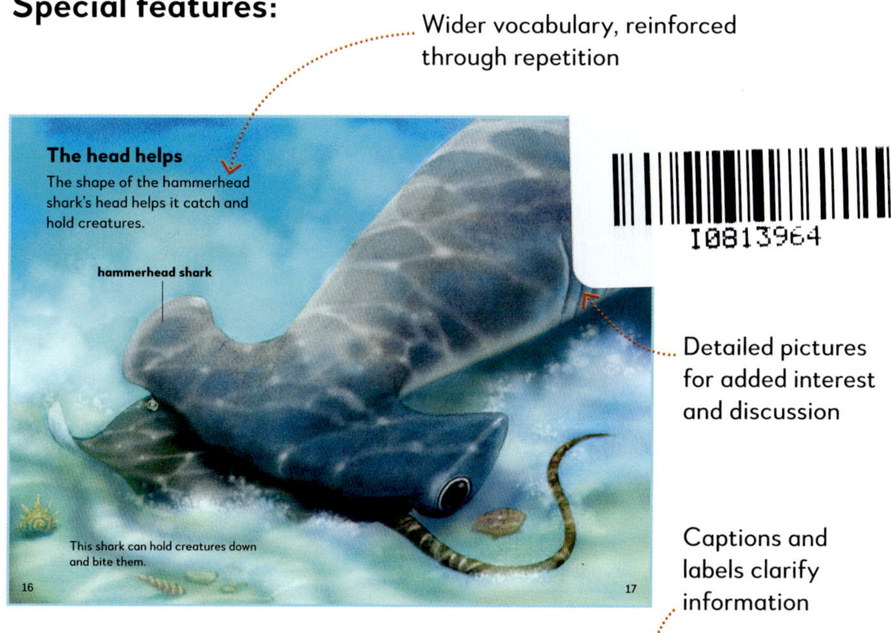

Detailed pictures for added interest and discussion

Captions and labels clarify information

Longer sentences

Ladybird

Educational Consultants: Geraldine Taylor and James Clements
Book Banding Consultant: Kate Ruttle
Subject Consultant: Dr Kim Dennis-Bryan

LADYBIRD BOOKS

UK | USA | Canada | Ireland | Australia
India | New Zealand | South Africa

Ladybird Books is part of the Penguin Random House group of companies whose addresses can be found at global.penguinrandomhouse.com.

www.penguin.co.uk   www.puffin.co.uk   www.ladybird.co.uk

First published 2015
This edition published 2024
003

Written by Chris Baker

Illustrations by Daniel Howarth

Printed in Dubai

The authorized representative in the EEA is Penguin Random House Ireland, Morrison Chambers, 32 Nassau Street, Dublin D02 YH68

A CIP catalogue record for this book is available from the British Library

ISBN: 978-0-241-56369-4

All correspondence to:
Ladybird Books
Penguin Random House Children's
One Embassy Gardens, 8 Viaduct Gardens, London SW11 7BW

Written by Chris Baker
Illustrated by Daniel Howarth

Contents

Scary sharks? 8

Sharks that hunt 10

Sharks find food 12

Sharks catch food 14

The head helps 16

Shark teeth 18

Shark shapes 20

Basking sharks 22

Eat, eat, eat! 24

Basking sharks' food 26

Big and little sharks 28

Glow-in-the-dark shark! 30

Shark babies 32

Pups look after themselves 34

Shark journeys 36

Swim, swim, swim! 38

Shark attack! 40

Which sharks? 42

Picture glossary 44

Index 46

Sharks quiz 47

Scary sharks?

Some sharks have very big teeth and look scary.

Other sharks are not so scary.

Some sharks are very little.

Sharks that hunt

Some sharks, like the great white shark, hunt other big sea creatures.

Sharks look for food.

great white shark

Sharks find food

Many sharks can see very well. This helps them find creatures to eat.

The shape of a hammerhead shark's head helps it to see well.

Sharks catch food

When great white sharks see a creature to eat, they can swim very fast to catch it. When they catch food, they bite it.

This shark swims fast!

This shark bites its food with its big teeth.

The head helps

The shape of the hammerhead shark's head helps it catch and hold creatures.

This shark can hold creatures down and bite them.

Shark teeth

Great white sharks have many teeth. When a shark's teeth come out, it will get new ones.

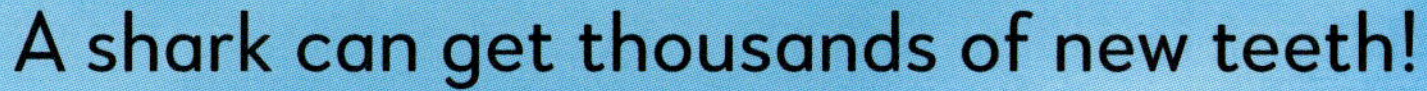

A shark can get thousands of new teeth!

Shark shapes

Many sharks have shapes that help them swim fast in the water.

This mako shark can swim fast.

The great white shark's shape helps it go fast.

This shark does not swim fast.

Basking sharks

Basking sharks are very big. They might look scary, but they are not.

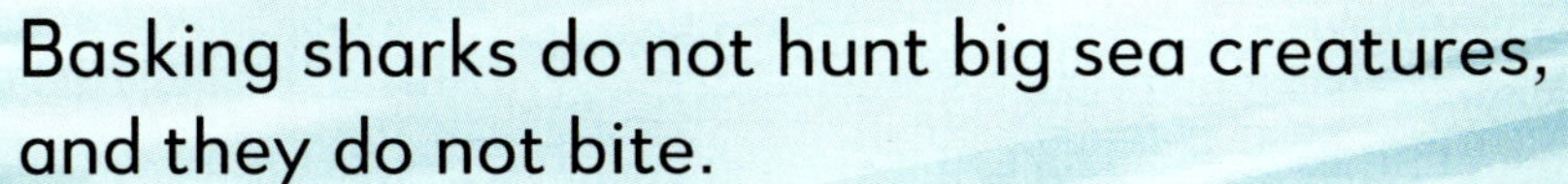

Basking sharks do not hunt big sea creatures, and they do not bite.

basking shark

Eat, eat, eat!

The basking shark eats little creatures called plankton.

Basking sharks do not have big teeth to bite plankton – they just scoop them up.

Basking sharks' food

Basking sharks are so big, that they have to scoop up and eat millions of plankton.

Basking sharks eat millions of very little plankton.

Little plankton look like this.

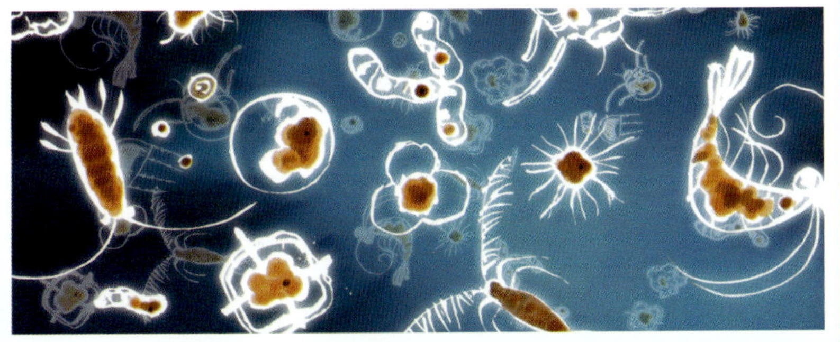

Big and little sharks

Some sharks are big, and other sharks are little.

basking shark

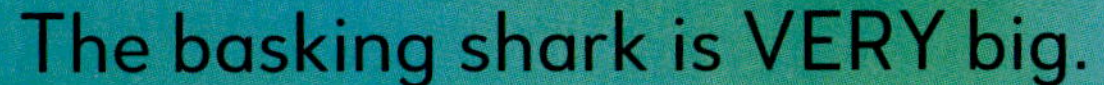

The basking shark is VERY big.

The dwarf lantern shark is VERY little.

Glow-in-the-dark shark!

The dwarf lantern shark swims in the dark sea where it can glow in the dark.

Shark babies

Shark babies are called pups. Some pups come out of an egg.

This shark pup comes from an egg.

Many shark pups do not come out of an egg. Their mothers give birth to them.

The mako shark gives birth to pups.

Pups look after themselves

When shark pups are born,
they can look after themselves.
They will swim and hunt.

These mako shark pups can hunt when they are born.

Shark journeys

Some sharks go on great journeys. One great white shark went from Africa to Australia and back.

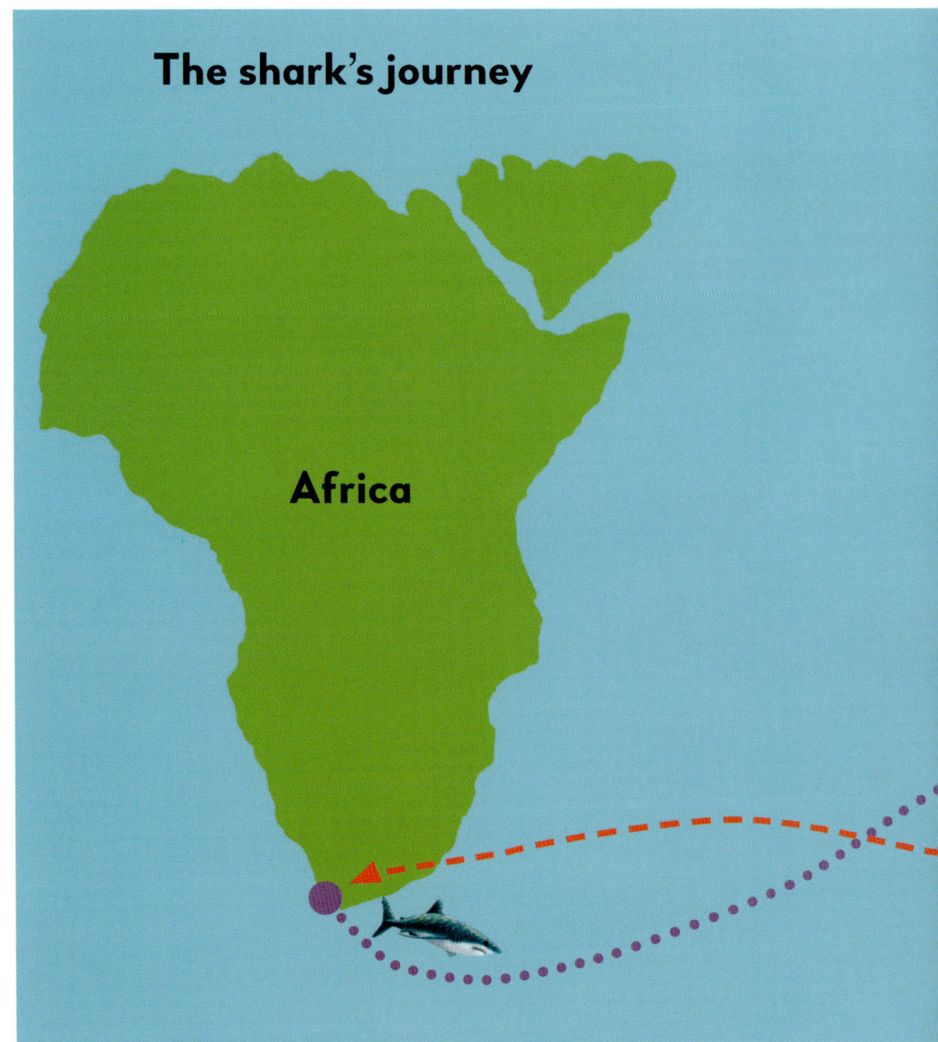

The shark went on a journey of nineteen thousand kilometres.

This is one great white shark's nineteen-thousand-kilometre journey.

Swim, swim, swim!

Many sharks must swim all the time. They can't breathe if they don't swim all the time.

These hammerhead sharks must swim all the time so they can breathe.

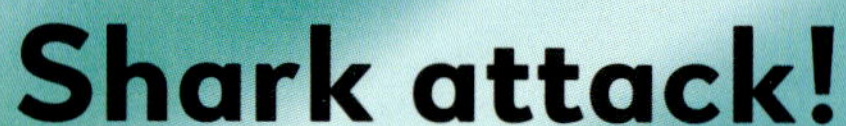

Shark attack!

Many sharks attack and eat other sea creatures. But sharks do not often attack or eat people.

Sharks do not often eat people.

Which sharks?

If you went down in the water, which sharks would you like to see or swim with?

The scary great white shark.

The big hammerhead shark.

The very big basking shark.

The little dwarf lantern shark.

The fast mako shark.

Picture glossary

basking shark

creatures

dwarf lantern shark

great white shark

hammerhead shark

mako shark

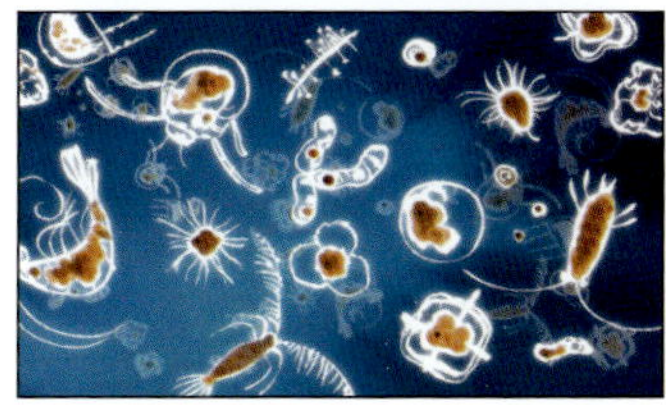

plankton

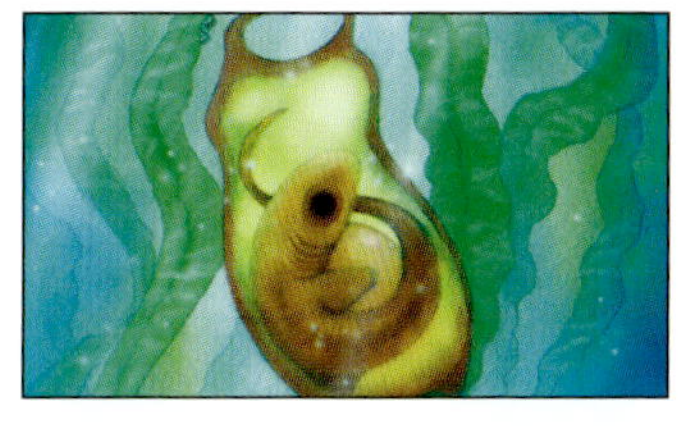

shark egg

shark pups

teeth

Index

basking shark 22, 23, 24, 25, 26, 27, 28, 29, 43

dwarf lantern shark 9, 29, 30, 43

food 10, 12, 14, 15, 26

great white shark 8, 10, 11, 14, 15, 18, 21, 36, 42

hammerhead shark 13, 16, 39, 42

mako shark 20, 33, 35, 43

plankton 24, 25, 26, 27

shark attack 40

shark eggs 32

shark pups 32, 33, 34, 35

teeth 8, 15, 18, 19